1000
REASONS
I LOVE YOU

1000
REASONS
I LOVE YOU

Rebecca Hall

MQP

Contents

Introduction

Why do people fall in love with each other? Scientists think they have some of the answers. Biologists claim that we're attracted to the pheromones of partners with whom we would have the healthiest babies. Sociologists point out that we pick women who look ripe for childbearing and men with sufficient masculine characteristics to appear good providers. But these theories fall far short of the vast and complex truth.

No one would deny that we form a host of tiny impressions, many of them subconscious, in the first minutes of meeting someone new. If the attraction is there, and the timing is right, it may or may not develop into love. What tips the balance? We don't love people for being perfect, but for the flaws, quirks, and idiosyncrasies that make them human. Vulnerability is more lovable than strength; clumsiness is much more endearing than gracefulness.

Real, lasting love is a two-way street. It has to be beneficial for both partners. There has to be a connection. The whole process of falling in love and loving is addictive and time-consuming, and at times terrifying. You have to take risks along the way, but the rewards are enormous and life-enhancing.

Every single love is unique. If you love twice, three times, or more in your life, each will be entirely different. Romantic love has some common ground with the love we feel for friends, family, or children, but it's much more complex and harder to sustain.

Maybe it's a mistake to analyze love too closely. However, I believe that it's valuable to stop from time to time and make a list of the reasons why you love your partner, to remind yourself of all his or her great qualities. When you've made your list, I recommend that you show it to your partner, or at least tell him or her the reasons you've compiled it. People never get tired of hearing the reasons why they are loved. And who knows? You may find it makes the two of you fall in love all over again.

1

Love: Past and Present

When we met, I was
immediately intrigued by you
and wanted to find out more.
I still feel the same way.

*I remember
the first moment I realized
you were interested in me,
and what a thrill that was.*

"I knew **immediately** that I would find him **irresistible.**"

KATHARINE HEPBURN ON
MEETING SPENCER TRACY

You tried to sound casual when you asked me out, but I could tell from your eyes that you weren't.

When I gave you
my phone number,
you memorized it.

I can remember every
detail of our first date —
what we wore,
what we talked about,
what I was feeling.

I **always** smile when I think back to the **little ways** you tried to impress me.

On our first dates we talked and talked, each fascinated by everything the other said.

I was overwhelmed by the
intensity of my feelings,
but not afraid.

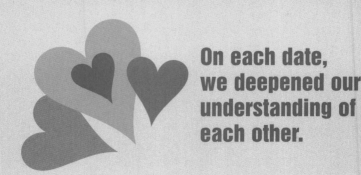

On each date,
we deepened our
understanding of
each other.

*You called me regularly, and
returned my calls right away.*

I could tell you had taken care with your appearance when we went out.

You thanked me after we had a great evening out together.

We never played games with each other.

You were **reluctant** to take things too quickly because you **cared** enough to get it right.

I couldn't concentrate on anything; you were always touching the edge of my consciousness.

We were nervous around each other, because already it felt different and precious, and we didn't want to mess up.

I was scared of love and put up emotional barriers, but you hurdled them with ease.

Secretly I remember the anniversary of the first night we kissed. I shouldn't think you have any idea when this was.

I became addicted to you, and got withdrawal symptoms when we had to part. I could tell you felt the same.

You gave me sweet kisses that made my heart jump, and strokes and hugs — all for nothing.

I never played **hard to get** with you, because I didn't **want** to hurt your feelings.

"Thousands and thousands of years
Would not suffice
To tell
The tiny moment of eternity
When you kissed me
When I kissed you."

JACQUES PRÉVERT

I **love** the fact
that you **wish** you'd
met me **earlier**.

We've **learned**
from the mistakes
we've made
together.

I loved unpeeling your layers,
        finding out bit by bit
        what makes you you.

I could see in your face and hear in your voice that you were sometimes unsure of yourself, and that made me feel closer to you because I felt the same.

I felt lit up from within when I was with you. Still do.

In the early days, I normally hold back a bit, testing whether I can trust the other person. I never did that with you, because you were so obviously sincere.

Falling in love is a leap of faith; I'm so glad we jumped.

You were able to make me contemplate a relationship, and made me love you enough not to walk away when things were tricky.

When I got **scared** and considered backing off, you **fought** to keep me.

Our first fight was **scary**, because I thought for a moment we **might** break up and realized **how much** I would be losing.

I used to give you little tests, and you would pass them with flying colors—unless you realized it was a test, in which case you refused to play.

The **first** time you told me you loved me, it just **slipped** out. I'm not sure you **meant** it to.

I felt younger and more carefree when I was with you, and people commented on how good I looked.

Loving you came **effortlessly**; I just had to **relax** and let it happen.

The first time you took me to meet your family, you were anxious that we'd get along.

It was achingly hard to say good-bye after a date.

I had never been treated with so much respect and consideration.

I used to **count** the hours until I would **see** you again.

You seemed proud when you introduced me to your friends.

You made me love you, even though I was very sure I didn't need to love anyone, and also pretty sure I wouldn't be able to.

There is something **bewitching** about our love, as though a sorcerer has cast a **spell** on us.

"Our **dreams** poured into each other's arms, like **streams**."

STEPHEN SPENDER

I never realized there had been an enormous gap in my life until you came along and filled it.

It happened all by itself, without either of us planning or expecting it, which made us believe in it.

The story of **our** love is as riveting as any novel, and only **we** know all the details.

The reasons I fell in love
with you in the first place
are different from the reasons
I love you now, but they're
all part of the same person.

*You were funny and
attentive, and I liked the
way you jumped from
one subject to the next
with ease.*

"We **attract** hearts by the qualities we display; we **retain** them by the qualities we possess."

JEAN-BAPTISTE ANTOINE SUARD

My first memories of you are a delirious blur, because you made me feel perpetually breathless.

It didn't take long until I **knew** beyond a shadow of a doubt that I wanted to spend the **rest** of my life with you.

There's often a tense, anxious period when you know you love someone and you're not sure if they love you. For us, it was very brief.

All the plans you'd made, and the life you'd created, you were prepared to change to be with me. I felt the same.

We **always** lose track of time when we're together.

When I **try** to imagine what life would be like if we **hadn't** met, I can only see a blank space.

Meeting and falling in love with you is the best present I could ever have been given.

I wonder if you have **any** idea of how much you **move** me? Maybe you **do**.

"Till I loved, I never lived."

EMILY DICKINSON

You have an instinctive sense of timing, and you seem to know when I need another kiss.

I **like** the way
you **decorate**
a sofa.

We still have conversations about those early days: what you were thinking, what I was thinking, and when we first realized we were in love. It's a compelling subject.

When you load your fork with a tasty mouthful and it falls off before it reaches your mouth, I always feel a pang of love for you.

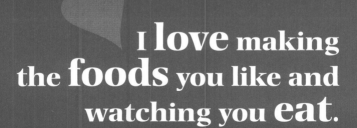

I **love** making the **foods** you like and watching you **eat**.

You're good at sharing — whether it's food, newspapers, or the space in the bed.

I like our conversational shorthand — the way we can understand whole concepts with one exchanged word.

When **you** come into a room, I'm instantly **more** alert.

"True love is above all an extreme form of awareness."

CLAUDE ROY

You're not good at sitting still for long; you like to keep busy.

We **prioritize** in order to spend **quality** time together.

We each like to know where the other is—not because we're mistrustful, but because we care.

It takes you an unbelievably long time to get ready to do anything, although you will never admit this.

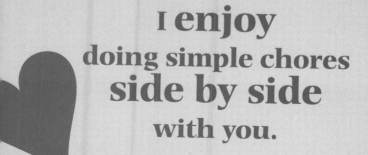

I **enjoy**
doing simple chores
side by side
with you.

We don't have power struggles, but we might play "scissors, paper, rock" to decide who has to get up and make breakfast.

I like the steady way you breathe.

I like it when you carry my bits and pieces in your pocket.

You talk to **yourself** sometimes and you haven't a clue that I **know** this.

"I see myself in you, and for the first time I am beginning to understand what I am, like a reflection in a spring."

KURT WEILL TO LOTTIE LENYA

You grumble silently when you're ironing.

The only thing you cheat at is dieting.

When my **feet** are cold in bed, you let me **warm** them on yours.

When you appear in my dreams, you're always kind, safe, and sexy.

I like the smooth,
   flexible way you move.

You're embarrassed when your
stomach rumbles in my company.

You listen when
I describe my dreams,
and try to suggest
explanations.

When you fall asleep in my arms, I feel an overwhelming rush of love.

I like it when you tell me your dreams; sometimes I glean extra insights about the way you're feeling.

You let me warm my hands in your pocket when they're cold.

You can fall asleep at the drop of a hat.

I miss you the **minute** you leave the house.

I like it when we **compare** diaries and **plan** our schedules together; it's symbolic of the **give** and **take** that's part of sharing our lives.

When I watch you sleeping, it's the calmest feeling in the world.

None of your bad habits are **completely** unbearable to live with.

I like squashing my face against yours.

We sleep with parts of our bodies touching. There's never a gap down the middle of the bed.

I like **laughing** with you **under** the bedcovers.

I like annoying you when you're reading the newspaper.

Sometimes we catch each other's eyes in the mirror when we're brushing our teeth.

Our late-night whispers in the dark make me fall asleep with a smile on my face.

You're groggy and incoherent first thing in the morning.

I adore the first kisses and smiles when we wake up.

You like rubbing noses —
Eskimo kisses.

I **love** the cute way
you **blow** kisses.

When you're not with me at night,
I hug a pillow. It's a poor substitute.

You're the **best** kisser I've **ever** known.

I love all the nuances and subtleties of our life together, the tiny acts of consideration, and acknowledgments of each other's needs.

This may sound spooky, but when the phone rings, I often know that it's you before I answer.

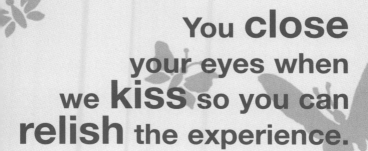

You **close** your eyes when we **kiss** so you can **relish** the experience.

We nourish each other—with food, refreshment, and emotional support.

You're tactile and good at affectionate gestures.

"I like not only to be loved, but to be told that I am loved."

GEORGE ELIOT

We're good at heart-to-heart chats.

We don't deal in "sweet nothings"; when you say something romantic to me it's sincere, not nothing.

You're reliable; you try to call when you said you would, and turn up on time.

I love the sound of your voice and all its different tones.

"To drink but once of her voice is to be intoxicated for ever."

LEONARD WOOLF OF HIS WIFE, VIRGINIA

I like chatting with you on the phone, and trying to picture where you are and what you're doing as we talk.

You give **crazy** attention to **tiny** things like buttering toast.

You make gentle fun of my messy ways.

You need your own space and you never cross too far into mine.

I love to see you all snuggled up in bed, waiting for me to join you.

We watch TV cuddled on the sofa rather than in individual chairs.

When we have a bath together, you scrub my back.

When we're sitting around at home, there are usually some parts of our bodies touching.

You are **extremely** appreciative when I **give** you a **massage**.

You're good at playing footsie.

I love it when you wash my hair for me.

2

Appearance

"**Wine** comes in at the mouth; **love** comes in at the eye."

HENRI MATISSE

Your eyes sometimes seem to look right inside me.

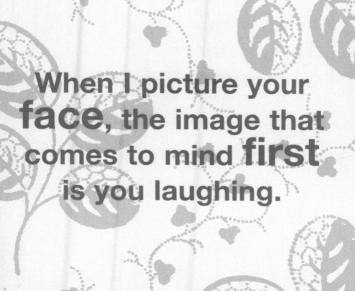

When I picture your **face**, the image that comes to mind **first** is you laughing.

Sometimes I get so absorbed in watching your lips, I realize I haven't heard what you were saying.

I like checking you out from different angles — in profile, from behind, lying down!

They say the eyes are the windows to the soul. I know what they mean when I examine all the little flecks of color in your irises and the emotion I can read there.

I love the smell and texture of your hair, and the fact you let me run my fingers through it.

I'd find it impossible to choose my favorite part of your body — there are at least ten.

"My love for you is mixed throughout my body."

ANCIENT EGYPTIAN LOVE SONG

Sometimes I have to resist the urge to **stare** at you the whole time, because I find you **SO** attractive.

You're very particular about your clothes, and I like it that you care about your appearance.

When that **special** sparkling smile comes on, I want it to be for **me** and no one else.

Your face **changes**; there are **subtle differences** from day to day and mood to mood, and I **want** to **memorize** them all.

You appreciate me and never forget to say I look nice.

I'm even **more** attracted to you now than I was in the **early** days.

You're **proud** of how I look and **that** motivates me to take care of myself.

Sometimes I know you're watching me when my back is turned.

Your **eyes** crinkle up when you smile, and your **laugh** is rich and infectious.

You can make me feel sexy, even when the mirror tells a different story.

You try to hide your physical imperfections from me, unaware that I love them best of all.

I'm relieved that you have physical imperfections, because it makes me less self-conscious about mine.

I like your ears and toes and knees and belly button, as well as your heart and your brain.

I love the scent of your body; it's distinctively yours.

You **don't** exercise to stay trim —you exercise because it **feels** good.

You use a polite smile when listening to people you don't respect.

Your shoulders are very comfortable for resting my head on.

We're exactly the right height for each other.

You can't hide **anything**; your emotions are written **all over** your face.

I like to smooth out the little groove between your eyebrows.

"At the touch of love, everyone becomes a poet."

PLATO

You have so many expressions and gestures, and I've learned to interpret most of them.

You've got the kind of face that will look even better as it ages.

I **love** the way you look at me, with that **mixture** of lust and love.

Photographs **never** capture your good looks **entirely**, because part of your **charm** is your animation.

I like checking out your toiletries—all the things you buy to keep yourself looking and smelling nice.

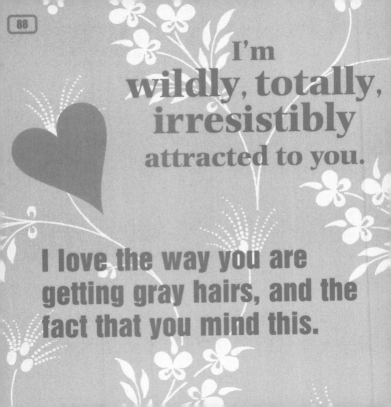

I'm **wildly**, **totally**, **irresistibly** attracted to you.

I love the way you are getting gray hairs, and the fact that you mind this.

I'm especially fond of the little place where the back of your neck meets your hair.

No matter **how** carefully you've dressed, there's **always** something a bit askew.

I **love** looking
at photos of us from
different periods,
because they bring back
detailed memories
that I can **relive**
over again.

I like dressing well for you.

I like the sight, the sound, the smell, the feel, and the taste of you!

There are clothes you keep for sentimental reasons and won't let me throw out.

The wrinkles you're getting are laughter rather than frown lines.

We borrow each other's sweaters.

You **care** about my opinion **after** you've had a haircut.

There are some **strange** items of clothing at the back of your drawer that I like to **tease** you about.

You're in touch with your male and your female sides.

We both **feel** much **younger** than we **actually** are.

Your waistline's a bit **thicker** than it used to be, so there's **more** of you to wrap my arms around.

I **like** running my finger along the **marks** on your skin where the elastic of your underwear has **dug** in. You **don't** like this.

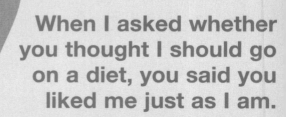

When I asked whether you thought I should go on a diet, you said you liked me just as I am.

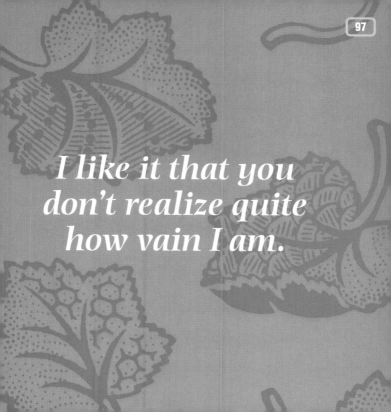

I like it that you don't realize quite how vain I am.

It's cute when you wake from sleep and your hair is all messed up and unruly.

Sometimes you think I'm wearing something new when I'm in a five-year-old suit.

I **love** looking at your hands and thinking about the **gentleness** they are capable of.

I like the **way** your feet **mold** their shape in your shoes.

"Your eyes are so **deep** that I **lose** my memory in them."

LOUIS ARAGON TO ELSA TRIOLET

You have
extremely
ticklish ribs.

*I love watching
you wash yourself
in the shower.*

When I'm buying clothes, I try and guess your reaction to them.

You **apologize** about your breath before kissing me if **you've** been eating pungent foods and I **haven't**.

Each little scar, mark, and bump on your skin tells its own story.

I love the color of your skin.

Mostly you tell me when you don't like something I'm wearing, unless you know I'm not in the mood to hear it.

I like watching you examining your face in the mirror as you get ready in the morning.

I like stroking the tender skin inside your wrists or at the back of your knees, or just beneath your earlobes.

There's a **vein** in your temple where I can sometimes see your blood **pulsing** through.

I can always spot you in a crowd.

You have a
fluid, effortless
way of walking.

"Most people look
at what is and never
see what can be."

ALBERT EINSTEIN

I like holding
your head
between my
hands.

*Your sense of style is
quirky and individual.*

On the whole, you like my style.

I always think it's endearing when you have a smear of food on your face.

You have dimples in the most unusual places.

I like to **lay** my head on your chest to **hear** your heartbeat.

You tidy my stray hairs and pluck pieces of fluff from my jacket.

"Love comforteth like sunshine after rain."

WILLIAM SHAKESPEARE

You notice parts of my body I've **never** given any thought to.

I could **never** tire of looking at **you**.

3

You—Young
and Old

"We love the things we love for what they are."

ROBERT FROST

With you, what you
see is what you get.
You don't have "sides."

*You are the kindest person
I've ever met, by a long shot.*

Your intelligence is as sharp as a laser beam.

I will never "possess" you, because you are your own person.

There's a vulnerability deep inside you that very few people see.

You have views on **every** single thing, and you are **always** sure that you are right.

No one tries to take advantage of you more than once.

You're very competitive, and can't bear to lose at even the silliest board game.

You're like a firework, exploding with brilliant and colorful ideas.

You never want to play me at the sports you know I'm better at.

Your generosity is **spontaneous** and utterly **without** calculation.

"My benevolent angel of balance, who chased away my dragon of doubt and lent strength to the lion of confidence in me."

SALVADOR DALÍ, ON HIS WIFE, GALA

You are brave about big things, and vulnerable about some odd little ones.

Whenever we've been in a frightening situation, you've always kept your nerve.

You're endlessly **patient** when you're explaining something I **don't** understand.

On the rare occasions when you get embarrassed, it's always over something that doesn't matter one iota.

You're very adaptable: You can make yourself at home in all kinds of circumstances.

It takes courage to open up to another person; thank goodness you were brave enough to do it with me.

I love your sense of adventure;
if there's a hill, you'll climb it.

Although we're **competitive** in private,
we present a **united**
front in public.

*If there's any fun going on,
you have to join in.*

Your occasional impatience is strangely endearing.

Being with you isn't always easy. You can be difficult and unpredictable, but the rewards are well worth the effort.

Sometimes you need me to take care of you, no matter how fervently you deny it.

I've never met anyone quite like you.

You're crazy and eclectic, but you've got your feet firmly on the ground.

You have a rich and colorful imagination, and you appreciate mine too.

You're a fundamentally cheerful person with an optimistic outlook.

You don't have a nasty bone in your body.

You have presence; you occupy your own space.

I love everything about you — even your bad moods.

I can't imagine you ever being mean.

You don't hold grudges; what's done is in the past.

You're mortified when you put your foot in it.

You have **plenty** of energy, and **never** complain of tiredness when there's something **fun** to do.

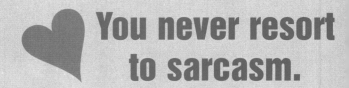 **You never resort to sarcasm.**

You're generally very honest,
but it's written all over your face
when you're telling a white lie.

*You're not always
as self-assured as you
pretend to be.*

**The last thing anyone could ever
accuse you of is pomposity.**

Your mind is working all the time, and I love it when you share your thoughts with me.

You're **not** arrogant, but **neither** are you self-deprecating; you're **happy** with **who you are**.

*You have a strong
sense of justice
and fairness.*

"You have been my
teacher, the **guide** who
led me through my inner
maze to **unravel** the
mystery of myself."

HENRY MILLER TO ANAÏS NIN

You don't **like** criticism but force yourself to **listen** to it.

There may be other people as kind as you, or as funny as you, but I've never met anyone who had so many wonderful qualities in one complete package.

In conversation, you can make the strangest mental leaps from subject to subject, and I like the fact that I can often see the connection.

You're **not** afraid of a challenge; I think you consider **me** to be a challenge.

You don't make promises you don't intend to keep.

You're always happy to change your plans if something better comes along, and I like that spontaneity.

It makes me smile when you can't manage something but are too proud to ask for help.

I've never seen you being patronizing.

You live in the moment.

"Love in the past is only a **memory**. Love in the future is a **fantasy**. Only here and now can we **truly** love."

BUDDHA

You actively enjoy life, rather than just get through it.

You believe in making the most of every opportunity.

Wherever you are, you never forget to enjoy the view.

Your lack of cynicism is refreshing.

I **love** your mind; it produces some **great** ideas.

You don't look back, regretting what's past and moaning about injustices.

I will never know everything about you; there's always more to find out.

You have a **genius** for living; I never met **anyone** quite so good at it.

When there's a puzzle or a riddle to solve, you'll keep trying long after I've given up.

You tell me the truth, even when it's not exactly what I want to hear.

You have your **own** interests and would **never** dream of giving them up for **me**. **Not** that I'd **ask** you to.

You have a good nose for sniffing out insincerity.

You've got way more common sense than me!

You don't take **things** too seriously— only **people**.

I love your enthusiasm; it's often contagious.

There's no bigotry in your personality; you treat everyone as an equal.

You'll take a gamble—but not with anything valuable.

Your compassion is **limitless**, and you never seem to **run out** of love to give.

I can't imagine you ever becoming jaded or world-weary.

You definitely see the glass as half full rather than half empty.

You have a **good** mind and you use it **well**.

I can't see you ever striking out at anyone, for whatever reason.

In a difficult situation, my father used to say, "Think of the worst that could happen and it probably won't be that bad."

You're the opposite. You think of the best that could happen and consider how to achieve it.

Your **mixture** of strength and gentleness is **irresistible**.

You have an enormous capacity to love and be loved.

I think you're the most upbeat person I've ever met.

You're **fiercely** independent, yet you **need** to feel **close** to someone.

When you're selfish, it's usually because you need more independent time and I'm happy to give that to you.

You don't always **think** before you **speak**.

You're not a complainer. If you're unhappy about something you change it.

You always stick up for underdogs.

Sometimes you wake up with a devil in you.

You don't hurry the good times; in fact, you're not a hurrier in general.

You're not self-deprecating; you're always willing to accept credit where it's due.

Some say, "Better safe than sorry."
You say, "Better to take risks than
be sorry you didn't."

You are the most inspiring person
I've ever met, providing the seeds
of some of my best ideas.

I have absolutely **no**
reservations about you.
You don't have **ulterior**
motives or **hidden** agendas.

I think of you as **sunshine** on legs, bringing **warmth** and **brightness** wherever you go.

"We throw ideas at each other, and each of us stands back, appreciating and producing ideas in their turn."

BEATRICE WEBB, OF HER HUSBAND, SIDNEY

You're perpetually curious about the world.

Quite simply, you're the best person I know.

When you're excited about something, I can imagine exactly what you were like as a child.

When you play with children, you get right on their level.

You're a peculiar mixture of young and old:
young in your spontaneity;
old in your understanding.

You are unbelievably cute in your junior high school photos.

You can be as stubborn as a two-year-old in a toy shop.

I hear you had your rebellious moments as a teenager. You still do.

You're a big baby when it comes to pain.

When I was a teenager, I had an **idealized** image of the person I wanted to spend my life with. **Thank goodness** I met you instead!

You talk to children as equals, and you listen to their responses.

I love hearing stories about what you were like as a child, and remembering what I was like, and smiling at the knowledge of the happiness the future holds for these two little people.

When we talk about the past, I describe it as honestly as I can, because I want you to know everything about me.

When you **buy** something you **wanted**, you're like a **kid** on Christmas morning.

You've got a
naughty streak in you.
I bet you were a handful
for your mother.

*I feel mad at any kids
who were ever mean
to you at school.*

Your mother did a good
job bringing you up; you're a
well-balanced adult, on the whole!

When I meet up with your side of the family, it's fascinating to check out the shared genes and the qualities that are uniquely yours.

When you've been away and I'm meeting you at the airport or the station, I get as excited as a schoolkid going to Disneyland.

Sometimes we feel like **naughty** children playing **hooky** together.

We can lie around for hours watching videos and eating popcorn like teenagers.

I wish I could take away
all the bad things that have
happened in your life.

We have snowball fights,
pillow fights, dares, double
dares, races, and competitions
over the most absurd things.

*Part of your charm is
that you've never really
wanted to grow up.*

4

Everything
You Do
For Me

You make me feel precious, cherished, and desired.

You're in my thoughts at least **half** of my waking hours. I **can't imagine** what filled **all** that space before.

Lying in your arms,
I feel **utterly** safe
and **at peace**
with the world.

'He who is in love is wise
and is becoming wiser,
sees newly every time he
looks at the object beloved."

RALPH WALDO EMERSON

You are the first person I want to tell when things are good—or bad.

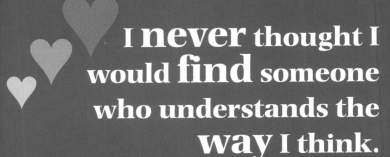

I **never** thought I would **find** someone who understands the **way** I think.

You make me feel as though anything is possible.

I wish everyone in the world could be as happy as us.

You've given a **structure** and a sense of **purpose** to my life that it **lacked** before.

Sometimes, unexpectedly, I get lovesick all over again, and that's when I know we are going another level deeper.

If I get shy in a roomful of strangers, you stick close by and make it easy.

You make me feel like the most special person in the world.

I'll never again be the same as I was before I met you. You've affected me.

"Love is but the discovery of ourselves in others, and the delight in the recognition."

ALEXANDER SMITH

You've made a **massive** difference in my universe; the horizon is **much wider** and the skies are **much higher.**

It's as though my luck has **doubled,** because I get to **share** yours as well.

You see me as a better person than I've ever considered myself to be.

I've become **more** assertive since I met you, because I can **hear** your voice in my head **telling** me I'm worth it.

You have a **great** sense of romance, and I love **all** the little treats **you** buy for me.

I love the fact that I can touch you whenever I want.

Your love can't prevent pain, but it's the best kind of painkiller.

It's always **fun** to **surprise** you with **kisses.**

"When you love someone, all your saved-up wishes start coming out."

ELIZABETH BOWEN

You make me feel calm when all around is in turmoil.

It's reassuring that you understand me so well.

If I'm seeing something in a **negative** light, you're good at showing me the **opposite** point of view.

You're the most
life-enhancing person
I've ever met.

I just like you
being around —
simple as that.

You listen to me —
most of the time.

Loving you, I feel **more mature**, as though I'm finally being **true to myself**.

You always make time when I need to talk.

Sometimes you **astonish** me by putting into words **exactly** what I was thinking.

The word *love* doesn't begin to describe the vast swirl of emotions I feel when I think of you.

You're my anchor—you keep me from going adrift.

I can often read between the lines of something you're telling me when you can't see it yourself.

I feel so lucky to be
part of your life,
to be accepted by the
people you care about,
and included in your
favorite activities.

*You've given me
confidence in my
own instincts.*

I can't think of **anyone** I'd rather have on my side.

You are **always** there when I need your help, and **never** make me feel embarrassed for asking.

It never fails to move me
when you tell me you love me,
no matter how casually.

My heart still jumps
when I see you, even
when I hear your voice
on the phone.

You care enough
to take care of me.

You never make me feel stupid, even when I make spectacular mistakes.

I'm more loving toward other people now; I feel as though I have an infinite amount of love to give.

You rub sunscreen on my shoulders even when I don't need it.

When I'm with you, I often think to myself how much I love you.

You hold me so tightly that nothing else seems to matter.

You don't provide every little thing I need. I'd suffocate if you tried to.

You seem to understand my train of thought when other people would be baffled.

Sometimes I still **watch** out the window when I **know** you're coming home.

You've seen the worst sides of me and you can forgive them.

"You have ravish'd me away by a Power I cannot resist."

JOHN KEATS TO FANNY BRAWNE

I'm glad you don't let me boss you around.

I've told you all the things I'm most ashamed of and, to my surprise, you're still around.

There are aspects of me that you alone see.

"She lov'd me for the dangers
I had pass'd;
And I lov'd her that she did
pity them."

WILLIAM SHAKESPEARE, *OTHELLO*

You persuade me to go places and experience things I wouldn't have done without you.

Sometimes I **feel** as though I'm going to **explode** with happiness.

You've **never** tried
to **change** me
(although there **are**
a few of my habits you
could live without).

*There's nothing I
would change about you;
even your faults are part
of the package I adore.*

My love for you changes all the time; as some aspects become less intense, new insights emerge.

I can trust you with anything—from secrets to money to my heart.

You **help** me to distinguish what's **important** in life.

You help me to **face up** to my fears and you **never** mock the irrational ones.

You can tell when I don't want advice, and step back to let me succeed or fail on my own.

I know how to handle you. Not many people do!

Your love isn't blind, but it's indulgent.

I feel more energetic around you, because you're good at motivating me.

You're **utterly** stable, like a rock I can **cling** to when I'm tired of **struggling** to stay afloat.

One of my favorite hobbies is earning your smiles.

You're a good influence, and you steer me away from my bad habits.

You let me get away with little white lies sometimes.

You're my security blanket, my emotional refuge.

You bring out the **best** in me.
Around **you** I'm happier, wittier,
kinder, wiser, and stronger than
I **ever** was without you.

*I get the best
of you as well.*

My happiness seems to
make **you** happy **too**.

"Love casts out fear; but, conversely, fear casts out love."

ALDOUS HUXLEY

You've made me like myself more than I did before we met.

I **never** feel lonely, because **even** when we're apart, I carry the **knowledge** of our intimacy **deep** inside.

You actually make me enjoy being unselfish!

You're my safety net, the one person I can rely on to catch me if I fall.

Immediately after an unusual event, I'll be going over the story in my head, figuring out the most entertaining way to tell it to you.

I now understand exactly what soul mate means.

You're **good** at looking at the **big picture.**

"Love cures people— both the ones who give it and the ones who receive it."

DR. KARL MENNINGER

They say that if you're lucky in love, you're unlucky at cards— and that's why I never play poker.

You make me believe that I deserve to be loved as much as you love me.

If I try to **pretend** I know something when I **don't**, you **always** catch me.

Until we met I never knew
I needed you, but now I couldn't
imagine life without you.

*I never believed
you could love me as
much as I love you,
but it seems you do.*

There's nothing you could do that would keep
me from loving you. It's out of my control.

One of the reasons I fell in love with you was because you have qualities I'd always wanted myself; as time goes by, I'm delighted to realize that some of them are rubbing off on me.

It wasn't my mind that decided to love you, and the heart is just an organ that pumps blood through the body. It was my soul that fell in love and loves you still.

You would never keep me
from doing anything I really
wanted to do.

"Life . . . only finds its
grandeur and its reality in
ecstasy and in ecstatic love."

GEORGES BATAILLE

I thought this kind of love
only happened for other people.
But when we met,
it happened almost effortlessly.

I'm your **favorite** priority and, when it matters, your **top** one.

Since we met, life has so many more possibilities.

Our love has given me a secret place to go in my thoughts, where I can always find peace.

You introduced me to a world
I'd never imagined before.

There are **aspects**
of me that **puzzle** you,
and I **want** to **keep** it
that way.

Every now and then, I deliberately
shock you just to watch the reaction.

"To be happy with a man, you must understand him a lot and love him a little. To be happy with a woman, you must love her a lot and not try to understand her at all."

HELEN ROWLAND

Sometimes you know what I need when I don't know myself.

You are always pleased to see me.

You know when I need to be left alone.

Sometimes I **watch** you and wish I could know **precisely** what it feels like to be **you**, in your skin.

You've made me interested in subjects I never cared about before, because I wanted to find out what interested you about them.

I couldn't bear to disappoint you or let you down.

When I ask you personal questions, you answer them as honestly as you can.

No one else has ever loved me the way you do.

You would never try to control me, because you want me to be myself.

I'm intrigued by you. I like being in new situations with you, just to see how you react.

You make me feel smart, capable, and occasionally wise.

You're good at telling me reasons why you love me.

You're not always sensitive to my needs, but you're receptive when they're spelled out in words of one syllable.

I know how to get your full attention.

Your compliments mean **more** to me than **anyone** else's.

I feel protective toward you. If anyone hurts you, they'll have me as their enemy.

I know you miss me when we're apart, because you call me about little things just to hear my voice.

When we're apart, I store up things to tell you.

I look on all sorts of things with a **fresh** perspective since you've let me **see** them through your eyes.

You always remind me to wear warm-enough clothes.

Seeing you vulnerable makes my heart ache.

Some of your advice is **planted** in my memory, and it helps me make the **right** decisions.

You **tell** me that I have
a **talent** for love;
I **never** did **until**
I met you.

Life would be **much**,
much harder without you.

You stop me worrying about
things that might never happen.

No one else would do as much for you as I do.

I **love** the person I **am** when I'm **with** you; you **bring** parts to the surface that were **locked** away inside.

You've made me satisfied with what I have instead of always wanting more.

I enjoyed my single days, but going to bed with you every night and waking up next to you in the morning is infinitely better.

You're the **only** person I know who **never** gets on my nerves.

I can be careless at times and it's nice that you're there, looking out for me.

I always **listen** when you give me advice because there's **always** some **wisdom** in it.

Life is more **intense,** colors are **brighter,** scents are **sweeter** since I met you.

You're my touchstone, my compass, my point of reference.

I like doing things to make you happy, like buying your favorite cookies or getting tickets for an event I know you'll enjoy.

You respect my dreams—even when you know they're unlikely to be realized.

I have never had to revise my opinion of you. You've never let me down.

5

Laughter and Tears

You are able to laugh
at yourself, and so am I.
This is crucial.

Sometimes I see you smiling
secretly to yourself, when you
don't know I'm watching.

You can make me
laugh at myself when
I'm in a grumpy mood.

I like the faces you make when your food is too hot, too spicy, or too bitter.

You're better at telling jokes than I, and you never mess up the punch line.

The way you sneeze makes me giggle.

You have a very cheeky way of winking.

You **laugh** at my **jokes**—and I **love** to make you **laugh**.

You **seem** to find me amusing **even** when I'm **not trying** to be funny.

Your silly voices always make me laugh.

I like to stand back and watch you when you're having fun.

You laugh at me when I mispronounce words, or choose the wrong word entirely.

Some of the pet names you call me are cute; others I'm not so keen on!

"In love, everything is true, everything is false; it is the one subject in which one cannot express an absurdity."

NICOLAS SÉBASTIEN-ROCH CHAMFORT

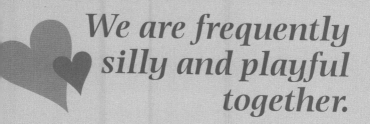

We are frequently silly and playful together.

We have the same sense of irony, and a whole library of private jokes that no one else would find funny.

We laugh together at least once a day, usually more.

I'm aware that you sometimes make faces behind my back.

I like the **funny faces** and **silly noises** you make to amuse children.

You **can** be **spectacularly** cheeky to me, but you **never** go **too far**.

Sometimes we have to clutch each other, we're laughing so hard.

When I tell a funny story in company, you laugh appreciatively, even though you've heard it before.

Sometimes a single word or catchphrase can set us off giggling helplessly.

My self-deprecating humor **annoys** you because you **don't think** I should be deprecating myself at all.

You love teasing me, but there are sensitive areas you know to steer clear of.

You tease **other** people as well as me, but **only** the **ones** who can take it.

Sometimes if I say something **cheeky**, you **kiss** me to shut me up.

You tell stories well, with **just the right amount** of detail to set the scene, and **not so much** they become boring.

We don't do that "couples thing" of interrupting and embellishing each other's stories.

You're happy to tell stories about your mess-ups and failures.

Sometimes we play crazy, make-believe games together.

You're good at using humor to defuse tense situations.

Everything is more fun with you.

I love playing practical jokes on you—you're such a great subject.

You make the same jokes every year at Christmas dinner.

We laugh at the same TV shows, stories, jokes, and life's comedic moments.

I laugh and smile so much more than I ever did before I met you.

I've been angrier with you than I've ever been with anyone else.

Even when I'm utterly furious with you, I'm still madly in love with you.

"Lovers' quarrels are the renewal of love."

TERENCE

I can never stay angry with you for long.

You don't **cast around** for **someone** to blame when things go **wrong**; **neither** do you **always** blame **yourself**.

After we argue, you skulk around like a disgruntled toddler until we make up again.

If I hurt your feelings, apologizing once would never be enough.

Even in a burst of temper, I can see your eyes softening when you look at me.

246

You're **capable** of apologizing when you **know** you're in the wrong, although you **don't** always do it.

When I'm furious and want to hurl insults at you, it's hard to think of any that are true.

You very rarely admit that you don't know something.

The one thing guaranteed to make you lose your temper is someone treating me unkindly.

We **argue**—of **course** we argue—but we can be **laughing** at **ourselves** soon after.

Our arguments start about one subject and meander through a few more, getting ever more ridiculous, until we have to laugh.

Sometimes you say black just because I've said white.

You have your cranky moments, and can be selfish at times, but I usually know how to deal with it!

You let me cheer you up when you are down.

When I'm sick, you spoil me rotten.

You don't always know what to do when I'm upset— but you do your best.

You hardly **ever** cry, but **when** you do, I **can't stop** the tears coming to **my** eyes as well.

When you don't feel well, you're as tetchy as a wasp in a jelly jar.

"Everything that irritates us about others can lead us to an understanding of ourselves."

CARL JUNG

When I look back, I can't remember the details of any of our arguments; good memories have taken their place.

You're a **sensitive** soul and you take it **to heart** if anyone is **unkind** to you.

You get in a sulk with me sometimes, but it never lasts too long.

Your little moments
of jealousy emerge
at the oddest times.

You never criticize me in
public, even when I'm in
the wrong, but sometimes
a particular look from you
will shut me up.

I get occasional **pangs** of **jealousy** when I **see** you talking to members of the **opposite** sex, but **then** I remember I have **no** reason to doubt you.

You don't say "I told you so" too often.

When we want different things, we can usually sit down and negotiate a deal that keeps us both happy.

We don't have huge, fundamental differences of opinion; any arguments tend to be about domestic trivia.

After an argument, we're good at sitting down and talking it through.

"Love is an act of endless forgiveness, a tender look which becomes a habit."

PETER USTINOV

"One word frees us of all the weight and pain of life: that word is love."

SOPHOCLES

You pretend you're not jealous when it's so obvious you are.

We're both pretty good at expressing our anger and clearing the air.

You **stand up** for **yourself** when you're treated unfairly, and you do the **same** for **me**.

You're good at listening to both sides before making judgments.

we **both** need to **pull away** sometimes, but **never** for long.

There are times when you don't want to talk; you just need a cuddle.

When I'm depressed, you don't tell me to "snap out of it," but try to cheer me up in the best ways you can think of.

When things are bad for you, I'm upset too, and I love you more than ever.

If something **bad** happened to me, I know **you** would be by my side as **soon** as it was humanly possible.

"There is no remedy for love, but to love more."

HENRY DAVID THOREAU

I love making up with you after an argument. It's utter bliss!

Living with you has taught me how to admit that I'm in the wrong sometimes— but not too often.

"Life is pain and the enjoyment of love is an anesthetic."

CESARE PAVESE

You usually know when to let things drop and not make an issue of them.

We never argue about politics—life's too short!

You walk away from arguments when you know that I'm tired and stressed; I need to learn to do the same.

During the **saddest** times, the **warmth** of your love **helps** me through.

You get very grumpy if I offer helpful advice on your driving.

We both hate someone peering over our shoulder, correcting our mistakes, and we try not to do it to each other.

We know we can lean on each other in bad times.

"The heart has its reasons, which reason knows nothing of."

BLAISE PASCAL

Neither of us expects our relationship to solve all of life's problems — but it certainly helps.

You don't turn molehills into mountains.

Arguing's not all bad. A discordant note can make the return of harmony sweeter.

We pull together when the going gets tough.

If I'm in an irritable mood, a sixth sense tells you whether I need a hug, to be left alone, to talk, or whether you can joke me out of it.

"It is very easy to forgive others their mistakes; it takes more grit to forgive them for having witnessed your own."

JESSAMYN WEST

You never shut me out for long. If something's upsetting you, I'll hear about it soon enough.

You let me freak out from time to time.

Nag is not a word we recognize — gentle persuasion, perhaps!

There's been very little that I've had to forgive you for.

If there's any distance between us, we try to meet halfway.

I've been infuriated, exasperated, and upset by you— but never bored.

6

Life, Love, and Friends

I like most of your friends, and they're all intensely loyal to you.

You can be the life and soul of a party, but sometimes you would rather be alone with me.

We **agree** on which friends we love **best**.

You think family is important, and I do too.

You're charming to **all** my friends, **especially** the ones you're **not** so keen on.

I can **always** tell when people are **boring** you — but **they** can't.

We both have friends of the opposite sex, and neither of us feels threatened by this.

I've never been embarrassed by you in company — only proud.

You're seldom rude to someone's face, but you can be amusingly honest in private with me.

You think the best of people, unless they give you cause not to.

You get affectionate birthday cards from people I've never heard of.

I don't envy **anyone else's** relationship; I'd much **rather** have the one I've **got**.

You encourage me to see my friends on my own.

I'm not the **only** person you **love** — there are friends and family too — but **I'm** your number **one**.

You have a charm that makes strangers want to please you.

I've **met** some really good **new friends** through **you**.

You've never been swayed by the crowd; you make your own decisions.

When you catch my eye
across a crowded room,
I know that you know
what I'm thinking.

You would
never let **anyone**
speak **badly** of me in
your presence.

Sometimes I like to sit back and watch you in company.

I value your opinions on people, because your judgments tend to be amazingly correct.

We had relationships **before** we met, but **neither** of us is worried about the other's **past**.

A couple of my friends are attracted to you and you've no idea.

You're good at getting people to divulge personal information.

I find it **hard** to believe that everyone who **knows** you isn't as **much** in love with you as I am — but I'm **glad** they're not.

You've become friendly with more of our neighbors than I have, and I'm not sure how.

I've never introduced you to anyone who didn't instantly warm to you.

I'm so proud of how you go out of your way to help other people.

You've got good manners.

You rarely forget to say please and thank you— except to me.

Your friends say I bring out the best in you.

My friends all **approve** of you, but it **wouldn't** change my feelings if they **didn't**.

You get on equally well with men and women.

When we have company, nothing is too much trouble.

When I meet someone new who asks about my partner, I'm always proud to describe you to them.

Our **basic** principles in life are the **same**.

You light up a room when you enter it.

You get along with a wide range of people from different backgrounds.

You are not afraid to make a fool of yourself attempting to speak foreign languages.

"If you **judge** people, you have **no** time to **love** them."

MOTHER TERESA

You're not afraid to stand up for yourself.

I like us being joint hosts; we throw fun parties.

When you take dogs for walks, you chat to them along the way.

My family irritate you sometimes but you've never let them know it.

You can never resist anyone collecting for charity.

You stick up for me in family squabbles.

If your **mother** gives you a sweater, you wear it **when** she comes to visit.

We've never been touchy-feely in public.

You've got friends from every period of your life—from school, college, each job, and every place you've lived.

We both believe in being discreet about our relationship and not discussing it with friends.

You get upset if friends' relationships break up.

We're good at making excuses when we don't want to accept invitations.

We have a "Let's get out of here—now!" signal that we use at boring parties.

I like telling friends about quirky little things you've done.

When there is dancing at a party, you always ask me first.

You would never complain about me to anyone else; if you're mad at me you tell me directly.

You're not embarrassed, but you think it's funny if I go wild at parties.

We would never treat each other badly, because there's too much to lose.

You're always willing to welcome new friends into our circle.

We would never put each other down in public; I hate couples who do that.

You're very good at saying the right thing to people who are in trouble.

You're a people magnet; friends come around just to chill out, and strangers corner you for chats at parties.

There are **your** friends, **my** friends, and **our** friends, and that suits **us** just fine.

We guard each other's secrets, and we'd never pass them on.

You've helped me to set boundaries and not to feel I have to be all things to all people.

You **remember** the names of school friends of **mine** you've **never** met.

You make great new friends wherever you go.

Your smile brightens the day for everyone you meet.

You don't let anyone walk all over you; that includes me.

We cover everything in our bedtime chats before we go to sleep.

Who's the boss? Sometimes you, sometimes me, mostly both of us.

"To love someone deeply gives you strength. Being loved by someone deeply gives you courage."

LAO-TZU

I like it when you fall asleep with your head on my lap.

We each think we are a better driver than the other.

You remember things I've forgotten, and vice versa.

You don't seem to mind my untidiness too much.

You're not as organized as you would like to be, but you hate it when I try to organize you.

You're happy to fix that broken item at home I've never quite gotten around to looking at.

When we're **out** on a date, the cell phones are **always** switched **off**.

We both watch over each other's health.

You're good at thinking of things to do on a wet Sunday afternoon.

Material possessions don't matter to you much—with a few vital exceptions.

"To live is good. To live vividly is better. To live vividly together is best."

MAX EASTMAN

Love is the **best** medicine for **all** kinds of ailments; scientists are beginning to **prove** it.

You can do a good, if absentminded, foot massage while we're watching TV.

Sometimes we overindulge and other times we go on a health kick, but we do it together.

There's **always** a **random** collection of **clutter** in your car.

" We both understand that we could not have found a better companion in life."

MARIE CURIE, OF HER HUSBAND, PIERRE

I like the way you rest your hand on my thigh when I'm driving.

You **hate** going **to** the doctor or the dentist, and put it **off** as **long** as you can.

Sometimes you fall asleep in front of the television and it's virtually impossible to waken you.

You're **SO** cute when you **waken** with the pattern of the sofa fabric on your **cheek**.

You're perpetually surprised when I tell you you were snoring.

When I stub my toe, you kiss it better.

When you've lost something, I can usually find it for you. It's nice to be useful.

Every once in a while you
do what I ask you to.

You hate being told
how to do things—
you would rather find
out on your own.

When we're **together**, at
least **one** of us remembers
where we parked the car.

When I ask you to do something you don't want to, sometimes you agree and promptly forget.

There are **days** when we **want** to hibernate and shut ourselves **off** from the world.

You can be slightly deaf when it suits you.

There are **times**, **especially** if one of us has been **away**, when it **feels** like a **first** date again.

We can sit in the kitchen and gossip till the cows come home.

"All love that has not
   friendship for its base
Is like a mansion built
   upon the sand."

ELLA WHEELER WILCOX

You make little snuffly, sighing, grunting noises in your sleep.

When I'm hurt, emotionally or physically, your sympathy is heartwarming.

If we were stranded on a desert island for the rest of our lives, I don't think we would ever run out of conversation.

If I want **kisses** when your mind's on **other** things, we **find** a compromise that **keeps** us **both** happy.

We have intellectual conversations about philosophy and art, as well as about the best way to make a grilled cheese sandwich.

Sometimes we have silences on the phone, when we just listen to each other breathing and neither of us wants to hang up.

Seemingly I talk in my sleep; you tell me in the morning what I've said.

I'm free to speak my mind with you— although you'll tell me if I'm talking nonsense.

You look at me directly when we're talking.

"Between whom there is hearty truth there is love."

HENRY DAVID THOREAU

I would never assume that I know what you're thinking, although quite often I do.

I melt when you reach out and hold me in your sleep.

Together we form our own self-contained unit, a little protective cocoon.

When I **call** you, I can **tell** right away from the tone of your **voice** if you're **alone** or if there's **someone** in the room.

We always have fun, because you know how.

I'm always interested
to hear what you
have to say.

*You think ahead for me,
and remind me of
things I'll need.*

**You initiate conversation
at least as much as I do.**

We're good at making an ordinary event into a celebration.

Since we've been together there have been some unhappy times, but basically we're content, and a lot of the time we're blissfully happy.

"To love and be loved is to feel the sun from both sides."

DAVID VISCOTT

We fit **well** in each other's **arms**, as if we were specially **made** for each other.

When you hold my hand, you hold it firmly.

We've never **slipped** into a **routine**, because we're **always** open to something **new**.

We never "fill" time, and we certainly never waste it.

We sleep very well together, and our bodies adjust easily to each other's nighttime movements.

We're good at being quiet and still together.

I like tidying your hair for you.

"We live in the complicity of solitude."

JULIA KRISTEVA,
ON HER HUSBAND, PHILIPPE SOLLERS

There are no taboos, no subjects we can't talk about.

7

Tastes and Talents

We have **special** places that are part of **our** romantic history, and we're **both** moved whenever we visit them.

You can gulp down a meal in twenty seconds when you're hungry.

You've **introduced** your **taste** to my surroundings, and they look **better** for it.

We both like flowers and trees, and beautiful gardens.

You'll try anything once to see if you like it.

All the annual **festivals** and **celebrations** have become **more** special **with** you to **share** them.

In some ways you're a creature of habit, but your food fads change from time to time.

When you're watching something you like on television, you go into a world of your own.

When you listen to music, you listen to every note.

You **think** couples who have their "special song" are **mushy,** but there's **one** particular album **you** play when **you're** feeling romantic.

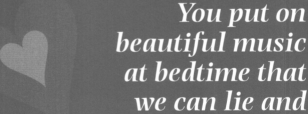

You put on beautiful music at bedtime that we can lie and listen to together.

You have the starring role
in my life — the center stage.

You dance or jig to
music on your own,
when you think no
one's watching.

We go for walks more
than I would on my own.

When I **read** a menu in a restaurant, I can **usually** predict what you will choose.

You're observant, and point out little things I hadn't noticed: a pretty-colored leaf or an oddly shaped cloud.

We're very glad we're not like any of the couples in sitcoms.

"The **purest** and most **thoughtful** minds are **those** which love **colors** the **most**."

JOHN RUSKIN

I like trying to identify the little songs you hum to yourself.

You appreciate the
little things in life —
sun sparkling through glass
or birdsong in the twilight.

*When we're
flying somewhere,
you offer me the
window seat.*

We like sitting outdoors
to watch beautiful sunsets.

Fortunately, we agree on our definitions of bad taste.

We like to sleep under the stars in summer.

If I buy you a present you don't like, you pretend it's just what you wanted.

You wear tactile fabrics and like me to do the same.

If there are **odd** noises in the **night**, you come up with the **logical** explanation.

You know how to receive as well as give.

You've **accepted** that it's **simpler** to let me choose my **own** presents, although you can **sometimes** be **very** successful with a surprise.

We get addicted to the same TV shows.

You urge me to try foods I would never normally go near, and some of them aren't bad.

You're always keen to try out new restaurants.

Before your birthday, you always try to find where I've hidden your presents.

You **know** the words to songs you **don't** even like.

You indulge my sweet tooth; it seems to amuse you.

You advertise your birthday **well** in advance, to make **sure** I don't forget. **As if !**

You always spend more than you planned when shopping for presents.

You sneak cookies and potato chips between meals, and think I don't notice.

Even if we have a terrible meal, or see a bad movie, we end up having fun all the same.

You laugh at
my gift-wrapping
skills.

Our **vocabularies** are
infectious; we **often**
adopt the **same** phrases
and **favorite** words.

I like buying unexpected gifts for your collections and hobbies.

You have a talent for **fun**.

We **both** like to **indulge** in a bit of **luxury**.

When I planned a surprise for you and you found out, you pretended you hadn't, because you didn't want to spoil it for me.

You **always** get me something **meaningful** on Valentine's Day.

We have the **same** taste in **most** things, but you **occasionally** come home with an item of clothing that **makes** me **shudder**.

You're an impulsive shopper, and you've made some strange purchases in your time.

You would never criticize me for buying something expensive—although you'd let me know if you didn't like it.

You never resent spending money on a vacation or a meal in a nice restaurant.

I love grocery shopping with you, but we tend to spend a lot finding ever more delicious treats to try out.

You're **good** at making **big** decisions, and **utterly** indecisive about **which** movie to **choose** in the video store.

I remember your favorite smells and colors before I think of my own.

You're good at remembering my preferences — foods, drinks, scents, colors — as if you carry a special list in your memory.

Would I give you
my last chocolate?
Yes, if you wanted it.

You **tease** me by
taking **ages** to open
packages, while I'm
waiting impatiently
to **see** your reaction.

You bring me drinks and snacks without being asked.

You **need** hugs as **much** as I do.

When we **travel** together, you want to **explore** as **much** as we can.

Sometimes you come and give me a second opinion when I'm shopping for clothes.

We **both** enjoy planning vacations, and have **endless** discussions about **where** we want to go **next**.

There always seems to be something fun to look forward to in our lives.

You claim you **never** eat candy, but it **disappears** anyway.

Our spiritual beliefs are similar and we respect each other's.

You have your crazy obsessions—I hope I'm one of them.

I love choosing presents for you, trying to find exactly the right thing.

You **never** miss an opportunity to **treat** me.

When I see a **beautiful** painting or a **glorious** view, I **always** think how **much** you would **enjoy** it as well.

We're both particular about how we like drinks prepared, and we're good at remembering each other's preferences.

When I **read** a book I **like**, I want **you** to read it as **soon** as possible so we can **swap** views.

You prefer to shoo insects out of the window rather than kill them.

You like **playing** in the snow and **baking** in the sun. You're **less** keen on getting **soaked** in the rain.

I enjoy the intimacy when you whisper your thoughts in my ear at an art gallery or in the theater.

You always yell at the top of your lungs when the water's too cold when you go for a swim.

I don't know **which** of us is **more** excited about **picking** out rugs and furniture for our **home**.

You put up with my crazy phobias and obsessions.

We like different movies but we're happy to watch each other's choices.

You're good at making a house feel like a home.

You **don't** put your **faith** in lucky charms; you **believe** in making your **own** luck.

I like it when we taste each other's meals in restaurants.

I know you don't miss your days of being single; you prefer to be in a relationship.

Sometimes we sit **talking** with our faces **very** close, and I **like** the fact that I'm breathing **your** air and you're breathing **mine**.

It was always important to you to find someone to spend your life with.

You have extremely good taste in partners—after all, you chose me!

You have hidden talents—not all of them useful.

You know about subjects I don't, and you're always happy to explain them to me.

I **don't** love you for your job **or** your social status; if these **changed**, you'd **still** be the person I **adore**.

Your curiosity about life and the universe is boundless.

The **range** of your knowledge is **broad** and **unpredictable.**

You think about current affairs and come up with your own opinions, rather than accepting the prevailing view.

You've got a great sense of rhythm.

I **always** want to know your **views** on a subject— **even** if I don't **always** agree with them.

You're not a quitter; when you take something on, you're determined to finish it.

When you disagree with me, I never feel as though you don't respect my point of view.

Your problems become **mine**, and **vice versa**.

You're ambitious, and you want to fulfill your potential.

We **pool** our **resources** — contacts, stamina, and money — so there's **more** to go **around**.

You would never stab anyone in the back, or double-deal to achieve your goals.

You're not afraid of hard work — although you're not very good at taking out the trash.

You don't **see** the pursuit of money as a **goal** in itself, but you **want** to earn **enough** for **US** to be comfortable.

Your sense of direction is better than mine—geographically and metaphorically.

You're endlessly receptive to new ideas.

You focus on one task at a time and give it your full attention.

Problems **never** weigh you down so much that you **can'**
appreciate a **delicious** mea
or a **great** piece of music—
and you're **teaching** me
the **same** talent.

You're not an excessive
worrier; on the whole,
you're fairly laid-back.

You're good at finding the silver lining in a cloud.

I've learned a lot from the way you approach problems (although I still think my way's best).

I like **watching** you when you're working with your hands, **puzzling** over a tricky task.

You boast about your little achievements but not about the big ones.

Neither of us resents the other's successes; quite the opposite.

I respect you **more** than **anyone** I've **ever** met.

You're interested in what I do and ask perceptive questions about it.

When I need advice on something, I usually ask you first.

You ask challenging questions and expect me to think about the answers.

You're good at remembering things I tell you, and asking about them at a later date.

You **think** I'm capable of far **more** than I would **ever** dream of.

"We find **rest** in **those** we **love**, and we provide a **resting** place in **ourselves** for **those** who love us."

ST. BERNARD OF CLAIRVAUX

When I'm stressed, you tiptoe around and make things easier for me.

You're **good** at making me **rest** when I've been **overdoing** it.

When there's a problem to be solved, we sit down to discuss it and reach the best solution.

You're more proud of my successes than you are of your own.

We're complementary. You're **good** at things I'm **not**, and vice versa, so **together** we're **much** stronger.

You don't fall apart in a crisis; you're the kind of person who copes.

I can't think of a **single** time when you've **admitted** defeat.

You talk through your problems with me and respect my opinions on them.

When I give you advice you don't agree with, you nod and do your own thing.

We have a rule that we never talk about work last thing at night.

You're proud of my achievements.

You're good at fixing things.

Occasionally you take on projects that are way beyond your capabilities.

At **work** or at **play**, you **always** give praise where praise is due.

When I'm **feeling** overwhelmed by a task, you **tell** me to take it **one** step at a time.

I can always tell when you're nervous, even if you don't let on.

You **care** about **my** ambitions and pass on **any** helpful information you come across.

It's **nice** when we **find** time to have a **lunch** date.

You're better than me at leaving work behind at the end of a day.

I hurry home from work, eager to see you.

We would each be prepared to move if the other got a great job offer elsewhere.

Although we're both proud of our careers, we'd put our relationship first if it came to the crunch.

You have a very entertaining way of expressing yourself.

I have to be strict with myself about the amount of time I spend daydreaming about you.

You don't often get uptight about things.

You're **multi**talented; there are **loads** of areas you could be a **success** in.

You're always understanding if I have to work late.

The best method of stress relief I know is to close my eyes and think about you.

You have high standards, but you're not an unforgiving perfectionist.

Either of us would do our **best** to **support** the other financially in **changing** careers or **starting** a business.

If you ever had problems at work, I would back you to the hilt.

You're articulate and good at making people understand your perspective.

When we add together everything you know plus everything I know, we're a formidable team.

8

Love:
Now and
Tomorrow

We're comfortable just being ourselves.

I **wouldn't** say you're low maintenance, but on the **whole** you're **easy** to be around.

I can tell what mood you're in within thirty seconds of your arriving home.

We have secrets from each other, but not important ones.

Sometimes **you** can tell **me** why **I'm** in a **mood** when I **hadn't** figured it out **myself.**

Who needs an electric blanket when I've got you in my bed?

You're **pretty good** at emotional communication, when you **want** to be.

We often say the same thing simultaneously.

"The courage to share your feelings is critical to sustaining a loving relationship."

HAROLD H. BLOOMFIELD AND ROBERT B. KORY

I think we're **both** reasonably **happy** with the **way** we **split** the chores.

You think of **ingenious** excuses for me when I **don't** want to **talk** to someone on the phone.

When we go for walks, we walk at the same speed.

Sometimes you hug me so tightly it would be impossible to slip a playing card between us.

You don't make a fuss about accidents like spilled drinks.

Running our home is a **team** effort, and if **one** person is **too** tired or **too** busy, the **other** steps in.

I love it when you hug me from behind while I'm doing the dishes.

When you leave me little notes about things like picking up the dry cleaning, you always sign them affectionately.

Sometimes I don't **consciously** decide that I want to hug you; my body does it **automatically**.

I know the best mood to catch
you in when I want to ask you
to do something.

*When I'm fretting, and
can't get to sleep, you
kiss my worries away.*

You're good at picking
up the hints that I drop.

You're **good** at planning **ahead** and booking **treats** for us.

I like it when you **kiss** me **unexpectedly,** for **no** reason.

You absentmindedly reach out and stroke me.

We're each roughly as house-proud as each other, although in different ways.

It **always** amuses me when you **rummage** through your **neatly** pressed clothes **trying** to decide **what** to wear in the morning.

When my hair blows across my face, you tuck it back for me.

You fiddle with my fingers instead of your own.

I can tell when you're dreaming, because you're restless and your eyelashes flutter.

You touch my body as if it were your own.

You know that a good conversation is worth infinitely more than doing the dishes.

You have an extremely sensitive touch.

I **love** it when you **kiss** the **tip** of my nose.

We enjoy the quiet moments together.

You **enjoy** teasing me with **flirtatious** behavior in the most **inappropriate** circumstances.

We like to lie in bed with our faces so close that I can feel the movement of your eyelashes on my cheek.

When we have staring competitions, I usually win.

You have a **great** repertoire of **affectionate** gestures.

If I'm fishing for compliments, I'll never get them from you.

You've got a **knack** of letting me know **what** you want **without** putting it into words.

Life **isn't** always a **rose** garden, but being with **you** makes it **easier** to deal with the **weeds**.

Happiness is relaxing, cuddled up together, after a hard day.

Money is **not** an issue between us; **we** have an arrangement that **works**.

You leave an item of clothing in every room when you get undressed.

Our time clocks are compatible— we like to get up, eat, and go to bed at the same times.

I like saying nice things
to you and seeing how
pleased you are.

You respect my
privacy and would never
look through my papers
or diaries.

I like the way you doodle.

Sure, you have irritating habits, but they're part of you and they make me smile rather than sigh.

You **never** read the instructions that **come** with a new gadget or machine; you're **convinced** you can work it out **more** easily by **yourself**.

It doesn't matter to us who earns more money.

You always thank me when I go out of my way to do something for you.

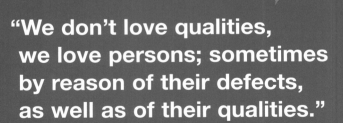

"We don't love qualities, we love persons; sometimes by reason of their defects, as well as of their qualities."

JACQUES MARITAIN

I relish our **quiet** moments together— breakfast in **bed**, curling up with a **book**, or just taking it **easy**.

I want you to feel good; I feel good with you.

You say,
"Waste not, want not,"
and **refuse** to replace items
before the old ones have
collapsed **completely.**

**"Love is, above all,
the gift of oneself."**

JEAN ANOUILH

Your **good** habits **massively** outnumber the **bad.**

No matter what you're doing—washing the car, painting a ceiling— you want to do it well.

You're **generally** appreciative
of the **little** things I do
for you— although there are
lots you **don't** notice.

*Usually you'll offer to
help me when I need it.*

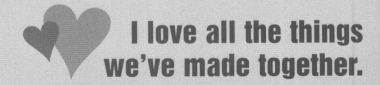

I love all the things
we've made together.

You get annoyed if you're clumsy, but not if I am.

You have learned **patience** in the **face** of my timekeeping.

We never subject each other to the third degree. There are much subtler ways of getting information!

We don't keep score of anything—whose turn it is to do chores, who wins arguments, or who spends the most money.

Whenever you **talk** about your plans for the **future**, you **always** include **me** in them.

I know you're committed to making this relationship work long-term. So am I.

"It's a funny thing about life. If you refuse to accept anything but the best, you very often get it."

W. SOMERSET MAUGHAM

I know you **well enough** to be **sure** that you will **never** deliberately **hurt** me.

Every day gives me a new reason to love you.

I don't know what the future holds, but I'm excited about making the journey with you by my side.

Being with you feels intrinsically right, as though it was always meant to be.

I am the yin to your yang; we balance each other.

We've both made certain compromises to be together and neither of us has any regrets.

Our **love** feels like the **arrival** of spring after a **long** winter.

I **don't** feel as though we're two halves of one whole. We're **both** complete people, but we're immeasurably happier **together** than apart.

Love isn't an instant recipe for happiness, but it's a great base ingredient.

We genuinely want the same things in the future.

We already have a gallery full of memories, which we add to regularly.

After all this time, you still keep surprising me.

We can be **together** and **separate**, each in our own little worlds, but always **united**.

There are no politics involved. We're different but equal, and we both know it.

I understand **why** people say they feel as though they **knew** their partner in a past life, but I don't **think** that's the case. We just **recognize** kindred spirits.

You know you can't take me for granted. And vice versa.

" We **survived** for the **best** reason of all, the **delight** of being **together**."

LILLIAN HELLMAN, OF DASHIELL HAMMETT

Our love is like a giant work of art that we are creating together.

**Every day
we learn more
about how to
love each other.**

For richer, for poorer, in
sickness and in health, I
know that you would stick by
me, and I would stick by you.

Neither of us is the other's
parent; we're each other's lover.

I don't **believe** there's only **one** person for **each** of us in the **world**. We could **both** have ended up with **entirely different** partners, but I **can't** imagine we'd have been a **fraction** as **happy**.

My love is like a river that flows steadily onward, and sometimes overflows its banks!

We've got a great chance of success because we're both able to communicate openly.

The more memories we create together, the more we'll have to talk about in our old age.

We're **independent** people who've made a **choice** to be **together**, and we **remake** that choice **every** day.

As **part** of a couple, you **still** have to make **some** journeys on your **own**, but you **know** there will be **someone** there at the end, **waiting** to welcome you **home**.

If we lost all our money, I know we'd survive.

"I could never love where I could not respect."

CHARLOTTE ELIZABETH AISSÉ

We both have our own paths; sometimes they drift apart for a while, but mostly they run side by side.

Some people **worry** about **losing** their freedom. I feel **more** free **with** you than **ever** before, because I'm **with** someone who **accepts** me just as I **am**.

No matter what happens in our lives, I will never ever be indifferent to you.

We go through **periods** when we're busy and distracted, and not **focusing** on the relationship, but it's **easily** strong enough to survive.

We take our relationship seriously; it's central to both our lives.

Sometimes I feel **insecure** about our love, **not** because you give me any **reason** to doubt, but **because** it's all so magnificent that **I can't** quite believe my luck.

"Grow old along with me!
The best is yet to be,
The last of life for which
the first was made."

ROBERT BROWNING

*I can't help worrying when
you're on an airplane or
driving long distances.*

If it was possible to cast a **spell** to keep you in **love** with me for the **rest** of your life, I **wouldn't** do it. I **like** it that you **freely** choose to love me.

We have several joint goals and ambitions for the future.

I genuinely can't imagine either of us with another person.

Our relationship isn't an institution with hard-and-fast regulations, but we have a mutual understanding that we won't do anything that could damage it.

"A **great** love is when **two** people manage to **support** each other **all** through life and **remain** devoted and faithful to each other."

KAREL CAPEK

Even if it all went wrong, I could never regret the time I spent with you.

We encourage each
other to strive harder.

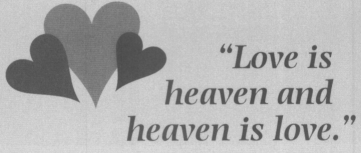

"*Love is
heaven and
heaven is love.*"

SIR WALTER SCOTT

We still have hot dates together—
I think we always will.

In many ways our relationship feels like a slightly naughty affair.

We each enjoy our own company, as well as each other's.

We're stronger because of the crises we've been through together.

We've both become more self-aware after seeing ourselves through each other's eyes.

Our **love** is the **best** adventure I've **ever** been on.

"If you aren't going all the way, why go at all?"

JOE NAMATH

We are each other's biggest fan.

We like being part of a couple and using the word *we* rather than *I*.

We **agree** on the importance of **fidelity**.

I want us to grow **old** and **eccentric** together, **embarrassing** our grandchildren.

We've had ups and downs, but it's always been exhilarating.

I know I am going to love whatever you become in the future.

You could say I've put all my eggs in one basket, placing all my trust in you; but it's a big strong basket sitting on rock-solid ground.

458

We **indulge** in working out the **details** of several fantasy **futures**: the **world's** our **oyster**.

"Love does not consist in gazing at each other but in looking together in the same direction."

ANTOINE DE SAINT-EXUPÉRY

Neither of us **resents** our **contribution** to the relationship. It **feels** pretty **equal.**

Before I met you, I could never have imagined how deeply fulfilling love can be on every level.

We've never lost the spark that ignites our flames!

We each look after ourselves, but have the other for backup.

We've made our own ground rules; they might not work for anyone else, but they do for us.

We've discovered that there are **many** different kinds of **magic** in relationships, not **just** the kind you **feel** in the **early** days.

We've put down roots in each other.

It's not **your** responsibility to make **me** happy, or **vice versa**. We both **know** we are responsible for **ourselves**.

There's nothing I would swap for our love—not unlimited riches, or eternal life, or a thousand wishes come true.

We **don't** analyze our relationship endlessly. "If it **ain't** broke, **don't** fix it."

There are certain memories I relive over and over, and I know I always will.

"When one stops wondering at the wonderful, it stops being wonderful."

CHINESE PROVERB

When I look back over my life in old age, I know I will see our relationship as the most important part of it.

We pack an extraordinary amount into our lives.

We both believe that love gives life its meaning.

There are **way more** than a **thousand** reasons why **I love you.**

Published by MQ Publications Limited
12 The Ivories
6–8 Northampton Street
London, N1 2HY
email: mqpublications.com
website: www.mqpublications.com

Editor: Karen Ball
Design concept: Balley Design Associates
Design: Philippa Jarvis

ISBN: 1-84072-533-8

10 9 8 7 6 5 4 3 2 1

Printed and bound in China